Crafts for Little Fingers

fun with
FABRIC

Annalees Lim

WAYLAND

Published in 2013 by Wayland

Copyright © Wayland 2013

Wayland
Hachette Children's Books
338 Euston Road
London NW1 3BR

Wayland Australia
Level 17/207 Kent Street
Sydney NSW 2000

Editor: Victoria Brooker
Designer: Lisa Peacock
Photographer: Simon Pask

British Library Cataloguing in Publication Data

Lim, Annalees.
 Fun with fabric. -- (Clever crafts for little fingers)
  1. Textile crafts--Juvenile literature.
  I. Series
  746-dc23

ISBN: 978 0 7502 7880 5

Printed in China

10 9 8 7 6 5 4 3 2 1

Wayland is a division of Hachette Children's Books,
an Hachette UK Company.
www.hachette.co.uk

Contents

Fun with Fabric   4

Finger Puppet Kingdom   6

Fun Felt Veggie Patch   8

Plaited Pals   10

Woven Art   12

Felt Pattern Book Cover   14

Sock Monsters   16

Button Buddies   18

Pom Pom Pals   20

Pet Pouches   22

Glossary   24

Index   24

Fun with Fabric

If you think having fun with fabric means sewing and stitching, think again! There is so much you can make with material, felt, buttons and wool without even threading a needle.

Small scraps of fabric, spare beads and buttons can be easily found around your home. It is a good idea to keep them all together so when you are in the mood to make something, you can find them easily. Try storing them in an old shoebox and decorate it in a similar way to the books on page 14.

To keep your crafts nice and clean, always work in a clear area and put down a table covering first, especially if you are using glue. Material is a little harder to cut with scissors than paper so ask an adult for help.

In this book, you will need:

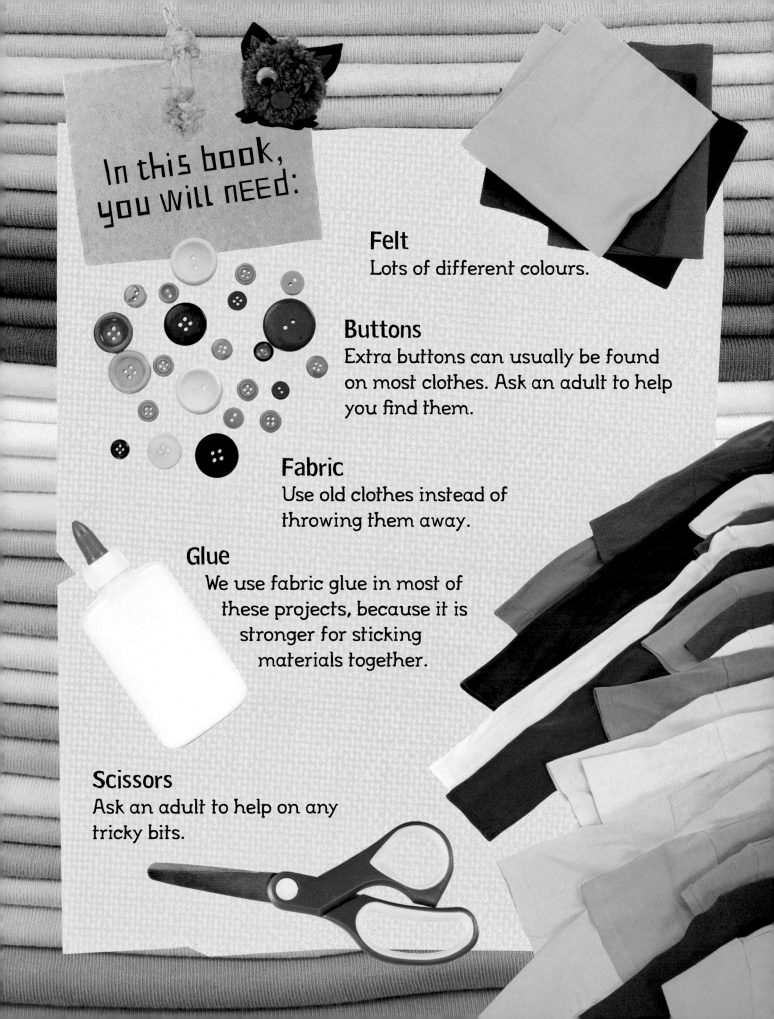

Felt
Lots of different colours.

Buttons
Extra buttons can usually be found on most clothes. Ask an adult to help you find them.

Fabric
Use old clothes instead of throwing them away.

Glue
We use fabric glue in most of these projects, because it is stronger for sticking materials together.

Scissors
Ask an adult to help on any tricky bits.

Finger Puppet Kingdom

Create a kingdom at your fingertips full of kings, queens, princes and princesses, protected by brave knights.

1

Draw your finger puppet template onto a piece of card/paper, and cut out.

2

Use the template to draw onto two pieces of felt. Cut out these shapes.

3

Glue the shapes together leaving the flat edge open so that your finger can be placed inside.

4

Cut out two circles for hands, two ear shapes and two eyes.

5

Make a king by cutting out a crown, red robes, hair and a moustache. You can cut out different shapes to make the rest of the puppets!

Once you have made one finger puppet you can make any character you can think of. If you are stuck for inspiration, think of your favourite story or nursery rhyme.

Fun Felt Veggie Patch

You will need:
Different coloured felt
Scissors
Glue
Wooden stick
Plastic pot
Googly eyes

You don't have to be an expert gardener to create your very own vegetable patch. These fun veggies are simple to make and even easier to keep!

1

To make peas in a pod, cut out a green ellipse shape and two thin curved shapes

2

Glue the wooden stick onto the middle of the green ellipse.

3

Cut out three light green peas and glue to cover the stick.

4

Glue the curved shapes onto the edge of the ellipse, covering the sides of the peas.

5

Glue the eyes onto the peas and leave to dry. Use the same technique to make more veggies. Roll some scrap felt into a pot to stand your veggies in.

Vegetables aren't the only things that can thrive in your soil patch. Try making felt flowers or felt fruit to plant!

9

Plaited Pals

You will need:
Fabric
Scissors
Wool
Glue
Googly eyes

Create these funky fabric snail friends with just some scrap material, wool and a set of fun googly eyes.

Cut three pieces of fabric to the same width and length.

Tie the three lengths together with a knot.

3

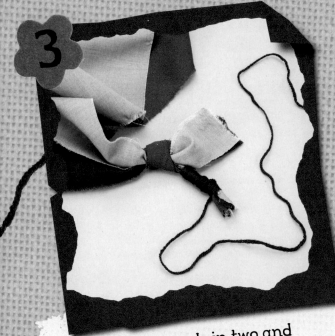

Cut the short ends in two and wrap each section with wool to make antennae.

4

Plait the long lengths together.

Try making a lovely, spotty ladybird or a creeping, crawling spider with this plaited pals technique.

5

Roll the plaited end up until it reaches the top and glue in place. Glue some googly eyes onto the knot to make your snail's face.

Woven Art

Have fun making this stunning woven art panel that looks great hung up on any wall.

You will need:
A4 size thick card
Wool
Scraps of material
Scissors
A4 black card

1

Cut triangle grooves out of the short ends of the thick card.

2

Wind the wool around the card using the grooves as a guide. When you have covered the card tie both ends of the wool together to secure it.

3

Weave scraps of fabric in and out of the wool until the whole board is full.

You can make many of these small woven panels, carefully remove them from the card loom and sew them together to make a cool rug or blanket for your bed.

4

Trim any long ends to neaten the weaving.

5

Fold the black card in half and cut a heart shape. Open the cut card out and glue this on top of your weaving to frame your piece of art.

Felt Pattern Book Cover

You will need:
A book to decorate
Different coloured felt
Scissors
Googly eyes
Fabric glue

Decorate your old notepads or school books with these fancy felt figures.

Your felt friends can be stuck onto nearly any surface by using your fabric glue. Try sticking them to bags, keepsake boxes or school folders.

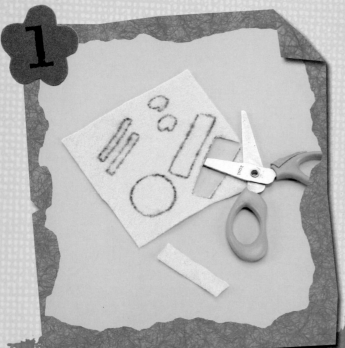

Cut a head, two arms, two legs and two hands out of some felt.

2

Cut a t-shirt out of white felt and cut out red lines to make the pirate stripes and red shoes and a pirate hat.

3

Cut out some brown shorts, a black eye patch and a silver sword.

4

Glue all the pieces onto the book using fabric glue and finish off the face with the black eye patch and a googly eye.

5

Surround your pirate with some yellow stars. You could create different felt characters for some other books.

15

Sock Monsters

Shape and mould your very own mini monsters out of old socks and pipe cleaners!

1

Stuff your old, but clean, sock with the cushion stuffing until it is nearly full.

Mini monsters can be made from any items of clothing you are about to throw out. Cut off sleeves from an old jumper and sew up one end, or stuff an old woolly glove.

Poke the open end inside your sock to keep the stuffing secure.

Tie a pipe cleaner around its middle to create a head. Glue two googly eyes of different size onto the head using some fabric glue.

4

Carefully cut two holes at the top of the head. Push a pipe cleaner through them to make some antennae.

5

Cut small holes either side of the sock monster. Cut a pipe cleaner in half and push a half through each side to make some arms.

Button Buddies

You will need:
Elastic
Measuring tape
Scissors
Buttons

Don't let the spare buttons you have lying around and hidden in drawers go to waste! Build your very own button buddy that you can carry around with you or hang on your bag!

Cut a piece of elastic about 60 cm long and fold in half. Thread the folded end through the holes of a large button and tape in place.

Choose ten buttons for the body and thread them on to the elastic.

Try making your buddies with different sizes and colours of buttons. You can take buttons from old clothes, but remember to ask an adult beforehand.

3 Thread about 12 buttons onto each strand to make the legs. Tie a knot to secure in place.

4 Cut a piece of elastic about 30 cm long. Thread about 20 buttons onto this. Tie at the ends and then tie it beneath the head to make the arms.

5 Glue some googly eyes onto the head to bring your button buddy to life!

Pom Pom Pals

You will need:
Compass and pencil
Card
Scissors
Wool
Googly eyes
Felt
Fabric glue

Create cute pom pom pals
for you and your friends
using scrap wool and some felt.

1

Use your compass to draw two large
circles of the same size onto some
card. Draw a smaller circle on each
and cut out.

2

Place these two rings together. Tie some
wool onto the circle and loop the wool
around it. Keep winding until you have
at least three layers.

3

Cut though the wool in between the two rings. Slide some wool between the card and tie a knot. Remove the card rings.

4

Glue googly eyes onto the pom pom. Cut some feet and a nose out of some felt and glue these on.

Don't worry if you don't have a whole ball of wool to use. Pom pom pals can be made using scrap pieces of wool to make a multicoloured pom pom pal!

5

Make some ears out of felt and stick them to the top of the pom pom with fabric glue.

PetPouches

Keep your treasures safe with a pet pouch. Decorate these simple drawstring pouches with your favourite animal.

You will need:
A rectangle of fabric (at least A4 in size)
Fabric glue
Scissors
Felt
Googly eyes
Ribbon

1

Make these pouches any size you like. Small pouches can be used to store jewellery or as party bags and bigger pouches can be used as a book bag.

With the fabric facing the right side towards you, put glue down one side and the bottom. Fold in half, press together and leave to dry.

Turn the material inside out so that the right side is on the outside. Fold down 2 cm of material from the top. Cut 2 triangles 2 cm from the edge.

Cut some features out of felt to make your animal. For a rabbit, you will need two ears, cheeks, whiskers, nose and teeth.

Glue the felt onto the pouch with fabric glue. Add some googly eyes.

Thread the ribbon in and out of the holes at the top of the pouch, and pull together. Tie the ribbon in a bow to secure the pouch.

Glossary

ellipse a shape that looks like a flattened circle

inspiration an idea that encourages you to do or make something

keepsake box a box where you can keep things that are special to you

technique the particular way of doing something

template a pattern used as a guide for drawing or cutting

weaving to make by passing fabric or threads over and under each other

woven a piece of weaving

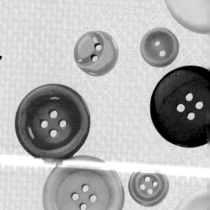

Index

antennae 17

Button Buddies 18–19
buttons 4, 5, 18, 19

cotton 18, 19

ellipse 8–9

fabric 4, 5, 10, 11, 12, 13, 22–23
felt 5, 6, 7, 8, 9, 14, 15, 20, 21
Felt Pattern Book Cover 14–15
Finger Puppet Kingdom 6–7
Fun Felt Veggie Patch 8–9

keepsake box 14

ladybird 11

notebooks 14–15

old clothes 10, 11, 12, 13, 16, 17, 18, 19, 22, 23

party bag 22
Pet Pouches 22–23
pipe cleaners 16, 17
Plaited Pals 10–11
pirate 14, 15
plaits 10, 11
Pom Pom Pals 20–21

ribbon 23

snail 11
socks 16, 17
Sock Monsters 16–17
spider 11

template 6, 7

weaving 12, 13
wool 11, 12, 20, 21
Woven Art 12–13